SCIENCE
MATH

DAWN STOSCH

mc **Marshall Cavendish**
Benchmark
New York

Marshall Cavendish Benchmark
99 White Plains Road
Tarrytown, NY 10591
www.marshallcavendish.us

All Internet addresses were available and accurate when
this book went to press.

Library of Congress Cataloging-in-Publication Data
Stosch, Dawn.
Science math / by Dawn Stosch.
p. cm. -- (Math alive)
Includes bibliographical references and index.
ISBN 978-0-7614-3213-5
1. Word problems (Mathematics)--Juvenile literature. 2. Science--Mathematics--
Problems, exercises, etc.--Juvenile literature. I. Title.
QA63.S76 2009
510--dc22
2008014557

The photographs in this book are used by permission and
through the courtesy of:

Images&Stories/ Alamy: 4-5, Brett Atkins/ Shutterstock: 6, James Watt/
Pacific Stock/ Photolibrary: 8-9, Stephen Frink Collection / Alamy: 8bl, Gelpi/
Shutterstock: 10, Louie Psihoyos/ Getty Images: 13, Mark Garlick/ Science
Photo Library/ Photolibrary: 14-15, Todd Marshall: 16, William J. Mahnken/
Shutterstock: 18-19, Thorsten Rust/ Shutterstock: 19tr, Salihguler /Istockphoto:
20bl, Petr Nad/ Shutterstock: 20-21, Gianna Stadelmyer/Dreamstime: 22,
Astrofoto/ Photolibrary: 25, Jurgen Ziewe/Shutterstock: 26-27, Mikhail Lavrenov/
Istockphoto: 28.
Illustrations: Q2AMedia Art Bank
Cover Photo: Front: Shutterstock. Back: UltraOrto, S.A./Shutterstock.
Half Title: Gelpi/ Shutterstock.
Creative Director: Simmi Sikka
Series Editor: Jessica Cohn
Art Director: Sudakshina Basu
Designer: Prashant Kumar
Illustrators: Indranil Ganguly, Rishi Bhardwaj, Kusum Kala and Pooja Shukla
Photo research: Sejal Sehgal
Senior Project Manager: Ravneet Kaur
Project Manager: Shekhar Kapur

Printed in Malaysia
135642

Contents

Water World

Scientists study the physical world—on Earth and beyond. Some scientists investigate ways to help athletes run faster, jump higher, and swim longer. Scientists tend to follow their interests, from improving computers to studying planets and stars.

Science is broken into categories. One of the biggest categories is biology, the study of living things. Within biology, there are many branches. **Marine biology**, for example, is the study of living things in water. Marine biologists use math in their work. They make many kinds of measures to keep track of facts and prove the truth of new ideas.

▶ Marine biologists count fish and other marine life, to keep track of the undersea population.

Calculation Station

One well-known public aquarium needed 5.7 million gallons of water to fill its tanks. To haul the water, trucks holding 500 gallons of water each were used. How many truckloads were needed to fill the aquarium?

To make the saltwater in the aquarium, 27 truckloads of table salt were needed. If each truckload held 100 pounds (45 kilograms) of salt, how much salt was needed, in pounds? (Answers are on page 31.)

Fishing for Answers

Some marine biologists work in the "field"—in lakes, rivers, and oceans. Others work at aquariums. Those who dive into the deepest waters have to take air tanks with them. Sometimes, they must use underwater vehicles to protect themselves against the weight of the water. Math helps these scientists figure out how much air to take in tanks. They use math to calculate the water pressure at different depths.

At aquariums, scientists study and care for the creatures. To give the animals the proper care, marine biologists are constantly measuring and weighing things. They need to figure out how much food the animals need. They have to make sure the water has the right balance of salt.

Big as a Whale

One type of animal that marine biologists study is whales, which are some of the largest creatures on Earth. The scientists have to measure these huge animals, and it is not easy. Orca whales, for instance, are about 19 feet (6 meters) long. They weigh around 10,000 pounds (4,536 kg). Baby orca whales, or calves, are about 140 pounds (64 kg). The largest animal on Earth, the blue whale, can grow to be 110 feet (34 m) long. That is as long as three school buses and bigger than even the biggest dinosaur.

In the Mouth of a Whale

Scientists use **logic** to sort the creatures into divisions that make sense. Logic is the science of correct reasoning. It is how we make sense of the world. Logic is the heart of math.

For instance, scientists have found that whales can be logically divided into two groups, based on how the creatures eat. One kind of whale has **baleen** in its mouth. Those are strips of material that are like the material in an animal horn. The strips act in the same way a kitchen strainer does. The strips separate small sea creatures, called **krill**, from the ocean water.

The other kind of whale has teeth to catch and rip food. Toothed whales eat their food whole. They use their teeth mainly for tearing. Most toothed whales eat fish, **plankton**, and krill. They also eat other animals, such as birds and seals.

▼ Humpbacks can weigh 35 to 40 tons.

Hands-On Math

Whales are some of the biggest mammals on Earth. Although we know that whales are huge, it can be hard to imagine how big they really are. You can get a better idea by comparing them to something else—like you!

What You Will Need:

- 1-inch grid paper
- Measuring tape, best if 6 feet or longer
- Different colored pens or pencils
- Table of whale lengths, provided
- Tape

Humpback	40 feet
Sperm	60 feet
Blue	90 feet
Beluga	12 feet

What to Do:

1 Measure your height by putting a pencil mark on a wall and measuring up from the ground. Round that number to the nearest foot.

2 One inch on the grid paper will equal one foot in actual length. Choose a whale from the table and shade in its relative length on the paper. For example, a whale that is 40 feet long would be 40 inches on the grid paper, to the nearest foot.

3 Shade in your length at the bottom of the grid paper. Make yours a darker shade than you used for the whale (hint: use two different colored pens or pencils). Again, let one inch equal one foot, to the nearest foot.

4 Repeat the steps with the sperm whale, and then with the blue and beluga whales.

Explain Away

For each whale, think about how many of "you" are needed to be as long as the whale. Divide your height, in feet, into each whale length, in feet. (Answer is on page 31).

Sharks in the Water

Sharks have long fascinated scientists. Sharks range in size from the very smallest, the **pygmy** shark, to the very largest, the whale shark. The **pygmy** shark is less than a foot (22 centimeters) long. The whale shark can be up to 40 feet long (12 m). It can weigh more than 15 tons.

Sharks are a type of fish. They are shaped like many of the fish you would have in a tank at home—just larger. The whale shark is the biggest shark, and therefore the biggest fish, in the oceans. It is not a whale, despite its name. The creature is called a whale because of its large size. Whales use blowholes to breathe oxygen from the air. Whale sharks do not. Sharks have gills on the side of their heads. They get their oxygen from the water.

Facts to Bite Into

A shark's main defense is its teeth, but it keeps losing them! A shark can grow up to 30,000 teeth in its lifetime. Sharks usually lose a complete row of teeth every eight days. When a shark loses a tooth, a new one grows right away.

Sharks use those teeth to eat lots of food, though not as much as you might think. Sharks eat food daily equal to about 2 percent of their body weight. Humans tend to eat a bit more than that in relation to their body weight. Fast-moving sharks eat creatures such as fish, squid, other sharks, sea lions, seals, and even small whales. Bottom-dwelling sharks eat crabs and clams from the ocean floor. Sharks known as **filter feeders**, which are the largest sharks, eat the tiniest items in the sea: plankton.

Calculation Station

In one area of the ocean, there are five mako sharks. Let's see how many pounds of food they eat. They feed on the tropical fish around them. Three of the sharks weigh 110 pounds, and two weigh 70 pounds. The bigger sharks each eat 2 pounds of food a day, and the slightly smaller sharks each eat 1.5 pounds of food a day. How many pounds of fish will they have eaten in a two-week period? (Answer is on page 31.)

◀ Whale sharks weigh between 13 to 20 tons.

Dolphin Delights

Scientists study dolphins and find them to be friendly animals to work with. Dolphins often seem to like human companionship. These sea mammals are easily trained.

A dolphin is actually a toothed whale. Dolphins can grow to be over 20 feet (6 m) long, though the average is more like 8 to 13 feet (2 to 4 m) long. The creatures are often confused with porpoises, which are smaller. One way to tell the two apart is to look at their heads. Porpoises have beaks, and dolphins do not.

Eating and Breathing

Dolphins eat their food live, except when trained to eat otherwise. Their primary food is fish, such as herring, mackerel, and sardines. Some kinds of dolphins seem to like squid and shrimp. Shells have been found in their stomachs, too.

The bottlenose dolphin can grow to over 9 feet (3 m) in length. It can weigh more than 400 pounds (181 kg).

Bottlenose dolphins eat about 5 percent of their body weight a day. That means a 400-pound(181-kg) dolphin would need to eat 20 pounds (9 kg) of food a day.

Like other whales, these creatures breathe through blowholes on the tops of their heads.

▲ Dolpins can go up to ten minutes between breaths.

Hands-On Math

Dolphins and fish are both aquatic animals. Yet dolphins are mammals, and fish are not. Let's compare these kinds of animals, using a Venn diagram and a chart of their features.

What You Will Need:

- Dolphin and fish comparison chart, provided
- Paper
- Pencil

Dolphin	Fish
Threatened by human fishing	Threatened by human fishing
Warm-blooded	Cold-blooded
Will die if kept out of water	Will die if kept out of water
Take care of their young	Do not take care of their young
Smooth skin	Scaly skin
Some make sounds	Some make sounds
Blowhole on top of head	Gills on side of head
Found in fresh water and salt water	Found in fresh water and salt water
Get oxygen from air	Get oxygen from water
Swim in pods	Swim in schools

What to Do:

1 Read the chart.

2 Copy the Venn diagram on your paper.

3 Write all of the dolphin-only characteristics in the dolphin side.

4 Write all of the fish-only characteristics in the fish side.

5 Write all of the characteristics both animals have in common in the middle.

Explain Away

What did they have in common?
(Answers are on page 31.)

11

Land of Science

Our oceans provide plenty of fascinating study. So does the land beneath our feet. Many important branches of science relate to the land.

Some scientists study rocks. Others look into the forces that make volcanoes and earthquakes. One important branch of science considers ways to raise food from the land. Some scientists become experts on land animals.

Past Lives

Paleontologists get to study forms of life that lived long ago—such as dinosaurs! To do their work, the scientists work with **fossils**. Those are remains, like pieces of bone in the ground or old parts of feathers. These scientists also work with **trace fossils**, which are things that show a living thing once lived in that area. Trace fossils include footprints.

These scientists use math to track their findings. They use math to measure the fossils and sort out the kinds of life that once walked on Earth.

Calculation Station

Suppose there were three *Brachiosaurus* living in a remote forest. Each dinosaur ate 450 pounds (204 kg) a day. Each tree provided 50 pounds (22 kg) of food. How many trees would need to be in the area for the dinosaurs to survive for three days? (Answer is on page 31.)

They Were What They Ate

There were many different dinosaur species on Earth over time. Some of them ate meat, others ate plants, and some dined on both plants and meat.

Over half of dinosaurs, 65 percent, were **herbivores**. That means they ate only plants. Because of their huge size, and the fact that a lot of plants were needed to keep them full, herbivores ate enormous amounts of food each day.

Each brachiosaurus (BRAY-key-ah-SORE-us) was thought to eat 400 to 500 pounds (181 to 227 kg) of food each day. Think about the bags of salad you might buy at the grocery store: Each one is usually 16 ounces, or one pound. Each day a typical *Brachiosaurus* would need to eat 400 to 500 of those bags of salad just to stay alive!

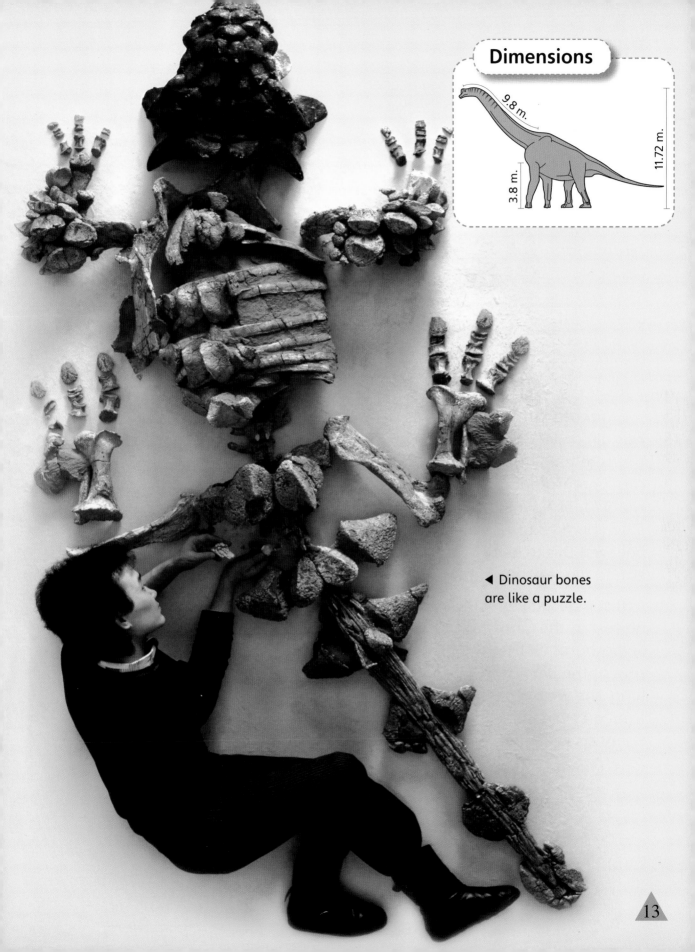

Dimensions

9.8 m.

11.72 m.

3.8 m.

◀ Dinosaur bones
are like a puzzle.

13

Big on Meat

Carnivores ate only meat. They needed strong teeth to bite through the skin and bones of other dinosaurs. Some carnivores had up to fifty teeth, and many of these teeth were more than 10 inches (25 cm) long.

For many years, paleontologists thought *Tyrannosaurus rex* (teh-RAN-eh-SORE-us REX) was the giant of all carnivores. *T. rex* weighed in at 6 tons. It measured up to 50 feet (14 m) long!

Giganotosaurus (jih-GAN-tih-SORE-us) was discovered in the late 1990s. The creature took the title of biggest carnivore from *T. rex*. *Giganotosaurus* was 47 feet (14 m) long and weighed a whopping 8 tons. Paleontologists believed this to be the largest meat-eating dinosaur ever to walk the Earth.

Just a decade later, however, the newest of the giants was discovered. *Spinosaurus* (SPIN-ah-SORE-us) stole the title of the biggest. It was 55 feet (17 m) long and weighed 8 tons. Will fossils from an even bigger carnivore be found? Scientists keep digging.

Chew on This

Carnivores needed a lot of food to survive. No one knows for certain just how much each of these dinosaurs ate. Yet paleontologists think a *T. rex* could bite off 500 pounds (227 kg) of meat or more. Weighing in at 6 tons, it probably had to eat a lot of small meals just to keep going. Or maybe it ate a few hundred pounds of *Triceratops* one day and then didn't eat again for a while.

◀ *T. rex* was bipedal. *Bi-* means "two," and *pedal* refers to feet. He ran on two feet.

Calculation Station

Triceratops weighed around 13,000 pounds (5,897 kg). If *T. rex* can eat 500 pounds (227 kg) in one bite, how many bites would it have to take to eat three *Triceratops*? (Answer is on page 31.)

15

All They Could Eat

Although most dinosaurs were either carnivores or herbivores, a small group were **omnivores**. That means they ate both plants and meat. Omnivores included *Ornithomimus* (or-neh-thoh-MIH-mus) and the *Oviraptor* (oh-vih-RAP-tor).

Ornithomimus was 6 feet (2 m) tall and 10 feet (3 m) long. It weighed 360 pounds (163 kg). Although this dinosaur had no teeth, it was still mainly a meat-eater. It usually ate small animals such as lizards, insects, and small mammals.

Oviraptor was another omnivore. It was 6 feet (2 m) long, 2-1/2 feet (just under 1 m) tall, and weighed about 44 pounds (20 kg). This creature had a mouth like a beak and two small teeth. Although it mainly ate eggs and plants, there are clues showing it ate small animals as well.

▶ This illustration of an oviraptor has colors you might see on birds today—but we can only guess at the true colors.

Compsognathus (COMP-sog-NAY-thus) was the size of a chicken.
Yet *Ultrasauros* (ul-trah-SORE-us) was over 100 feet (30 m) long!
How did the legs of those large dinosaurs hold them up?

What You Will Need:

- 4 bars of clay (4 oz.)
- 1/2-liter bottle (16.9-oz.)
- 1-liter bottle (33.8-oz)
- 2-liter bottle (67.6-oz.)
- Water

What to Do:

1 Fill the bottles with water.

2 Use the clay to make legs for the smallest bottle.

3 Try making each bottle "stand" on back legs. Then try standing the bottle on four feet.

4 Use only the smallest amount of clay needed.

5 Reuse the clay for the mid-sized bottle.

6 Repeat the steps for the largest bottle.

Explain Away

What did you discover about the legs you created for each bottle? How does this relate to dinosaurs and their bodies? (Answers are on page 31.)

Life as We Know It

Paleontologists study animal and plant life that lived a long time ago. They put together fossils like puzzles from the past. Many other scientists, however, study living animals. The study of living animals is known as **zoology**. The scientists within this field often become experts in one classification of animals.

A **herpetologist**, for instance, studies reptiles and amphibians. If a herpetologist and a paleontologist had lunch together, they might have a lot to discuss. The word *dinosaur* means "fearsome lizard," although research has shown dinosaurs might not have been reptiles at all!

Croc or Gator?

Many people cannot tell the difference between a crocodile and an alligator. A herpetologist could tell you the difference. The most obvious difference is the shape of the animals' snouts.

A crocodile has a V-shaped and very narrow snout. Alligators have a wide, more U-shaped snout. Because of the shape of their snouts, their teeth look different. A crocodile shows both upper and lower rows of teeth. An alligator only shows its upper teeth.

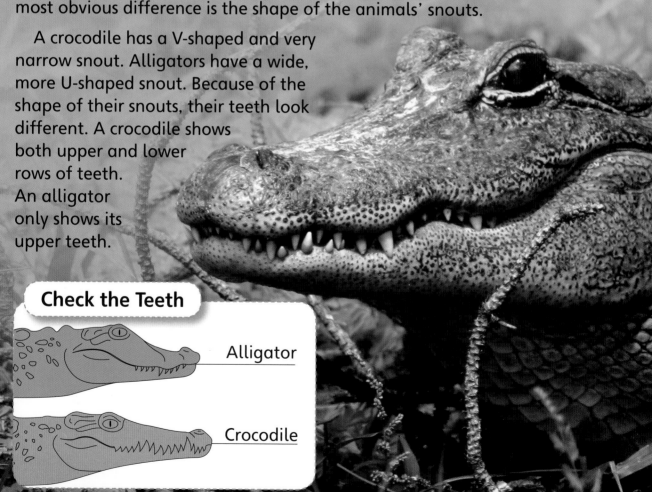

Check the Teeth

Alligator

Crocodile

Color and Size Assortment

Crocodiles have a lighter, olive-brown color to their skin. Alligators appear to be almost black. Crocodiles grow to be 19 feet (6 m) long and can weigh 2,600 pounds (1,179 kg) or more. The largest crocodile on record was over 28 feet (8.5 m) long. Alligators only grow to be about 14 feet (4 m) in length and weigh about 800 pounds (363 kg). The largest alligator found so far was over 19 feet (6 m) long. It was found in Louisiana.

▲ Note the narrow V-shaped shout and the skin color.

▼ Check out the skin color and the wide, U-shaped snout.

Calculation Station

Let's compare animal speeds in miles per hour. Alligators can run at speeds of about 30 miles per hour. Crocodiles can run an average of 12 miles per hour. Compare alligators to crocodiles. How far would each reptile run in 2 minutes at those speeds? (Answer is on page 31.)

Home Herpetology

There are many types of reptiles. Most live in the wild. Yet some can be kept as pets. To see what life as a herpetologist might be like, you can try raising your own reptile. You can use zoology math to keep track of how your pet grows and how you care for it.

Incredible Iguanas

One of the most popular kinds of lizards kept as pets are iguanas. These reptiles hatch from eggs. They start off small—about 6 to 9 inches (15 to 23 cm) long. They weigh less than a pound (1/2 kg) at first. As they grow, their size increases. They can reach 72 inches (2 m) long. They weigh 20 pounds (9 kg) and more at full size.

▲ Iguanas like to climb.

Stocking Up

Iguanas are herbivores. Their diet in captivity mainly consists of fresh vegetables, greens, fruits, and flowers. Feeding crickets or other insects to iguanas, as many people do, is not healthy for the creatures. Iguanas can get most of what they need through the plants they eat.

◀ Iguanas live 13 years on average, but they can live to age 20.

Calculation Station

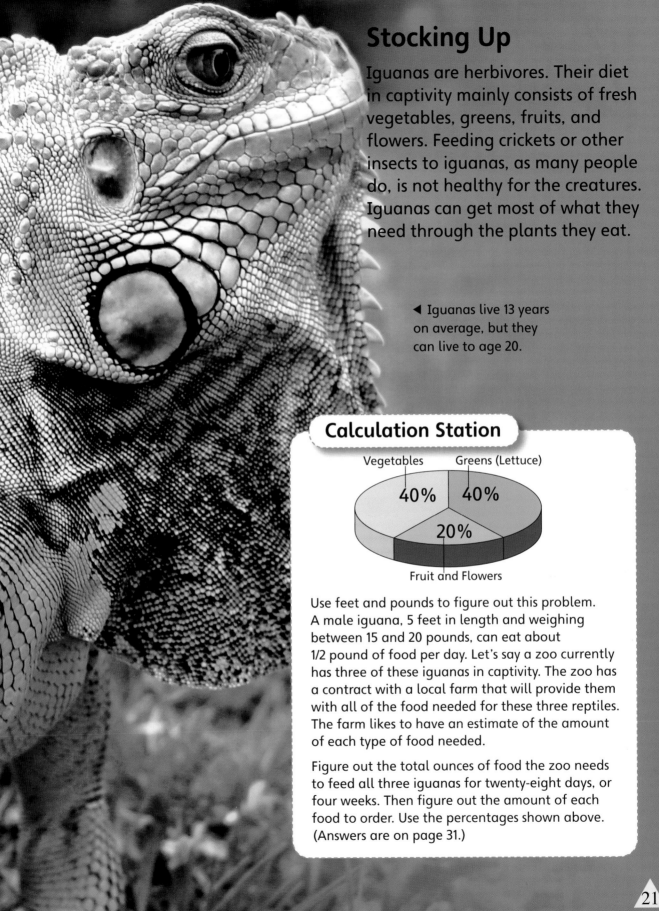

Vegetables 40%   Greens (Lettuce) 40%   20% Fruit and Flowers

Use feet and pounds to figure out this problem. A male iguana, 5 feet in length and weighing between 15 and 20 pounds, can eat about 1/2 pound of food per day. Let's say a zoo currently has three of these iguanas in captivity. The zoo has a contract with a local farm that will provide them with all of the food needed for these three reptiles. The farm likes to have an estimate of the amount of each type of food needed.

Figure out the total ounces of food the zoo needs to feed all three iguanas for twenty-eight days, or four weeks. Then figure out the amount of each food to order. Use the percentages shown above. (Answers are on page 31.)

Bringing Home Beardy

Another lizard growing in popularity is the bearded dragon. Although the name sounds scary, these lizards are gentle creatures. They can be great pets. They love attention and can usually interact with people rather well.

Bearded dragons are **hatchlings** at first. They are about 4 inches (10 cm) long when they come out of their eggs. They can then grow to be as long as 20 inches (51 cm). Although they look like they would weigh a lot for their size, bearded dragons weigh only about 2 pounds (1 kg) when fully grown.

Bearded dragons are omnivores. Their diet includes both plants and animals. Adults can eat about twenty crickets a day, along with a half cup of mixed greens.

Bearded dragons need space to be able to run and hunt the crickets. The minimum size of an enclosure for an adult should be 36 inches by 12 inches by 18 inches (91 cm by 30 cm by 46 cm). Not only do they need a lot of space, they also need a certain temperature. If the habitat they live in falls below 85 degrees Fahrenheit (29 degrees Celsius), the lizard will not want to eat and will begin to starve. Lighting helps keep the temperature right.

◀ Bearded dragons require hot temperatures to live.

Mary wants to get a bearded dragon for a pet. Her parents say that she will be responsible for all of the feeding costs, and they will pay for the rest. Her best friend, Pam, already has a bearded dragon as a pet. Mary asked her to keep track of all of the food she uses in two weeks.

What You Will Need:

- Calculator
- Pam's calendar, provided

			Week 1		**Week 2**
Sunday	Crickets	Day 1	23	Day 8	16
	Greens		1/2 c.		1/4 c.
Monday	Crickets	Day 2	19	Day 9	16
	Greens		1/4 c.		1/2 c.
Tuesday	Crickets	Day 3	25	Day 10	19
	Greens		1/2 c.		1/2 c.
Wednesday	Crickets	Day 4	17	Day 11	23
	Greens		none		1/4 c.
Thursday	Crickets	Day 5	24	Day 12	20
	Greens		1/4 c.		1/2 c.
Friday	Crickets	Day 6	22	Day 13	20
	Greens		1/4 c.		none
Saturday	Crickets	Day 7	27	Day 14	17
	Greens		1/2 c.		1/4 c.

Explain Away:

How much will the lizard cost Mary a month? If she gets $15 a month for allowance, will she be able to keep the lizard? (Answer is on page 31.)

What to Do:

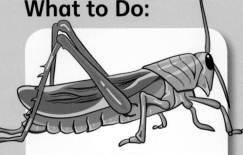

1 Find the total number of crickets.

2 Find the total cups of greens

3 Find the cost of the crickets: One cricket costs 3 cents.

4 Find the cost of the greens: One cup costs 10 cents.

5 Add the cost of both.

6 Multiply by 2 to find the cost for four weeks.

Sky Science

We've looked at scientists who study life in the seas and on land. What about creatures that live in the sky? Some scientists study birds. Others study insects. Yet these are really land animals. What about life beyond the sky and beyond our atmosphere? Is there any? Space scientists have found traces of water on other planets. If there is water, there might be forms of life. Scientists who study space, called **astronomers**, are discovering new things every year.

See It in the Stars

Ancient people looked to the stars and wondered what they were seeing. They did not yet realize that the stars are like the Sun, but farther away. They named groups of stars by "connecting the dots." They imagined drawing lines between the stars. They named the star group drawings for things that were familiar to them.

Ursa Major is a constellation said to look like a bear. People have been seeing this animal in the sky since the ice ages. Ursa Major contains the Big Dipper, too. That is a star group that looks like a huge water dipper, or scoop.

Angles in the Sky

Many constellations are made of polygons. **Polygons** are closed figures made from line segments that meet only at their endpoints; some angles in polygons are larger than 90 degrees. Others are smaller. A 90 degree angle, also called a right angle, is an angle that is like the corner of a piece of paper or a square. Lyra, for example, is a constellation that contains a **parallelogram**.

Lyra also has **line segments**. Line segments are straight lines that have two endpoints. Other constellations consist of only line segments and **rays**. A ray is a part of a line that has one endpoint and then goes outward in one direction.

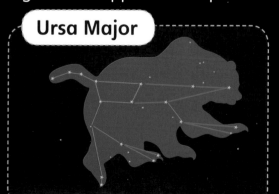

Ursa Major

Use a piece of graph paper to make your own constellation. Make sure your constellation includes at least one right angle. Remember: a right angle looks the same as the corner of a page. Make sure you have at least three line segments in your constellation, too. (Answer is on page 31.)

▲ Ancient people looked into the night sky and picked out interesting shapes among the stars.

Exploring Space

Gravity, the force that pulls other things toward the center of a mass, works differently when you are away from Earth. Each planet in the solar system is a different size. Each has a different orbit, or way of circling, around the Sun. Each has a different amount of gravity.

A Year in a Life

The length of time needed for a planet to revolve around the Sun is called a **planetary year**. Each planet takes a different amount of time to get around the Sun, so the length of a year on each planet is different. One year on Jupiter is equal to almost twelve years on Earth.

Imagine you just turned twelve on Earth; you would be celebrating your first birthday on Jupiter! The farther a planet is from the Sun, the longer its year will be, compared to one Earth year. A year on Earth is 365.24 days.

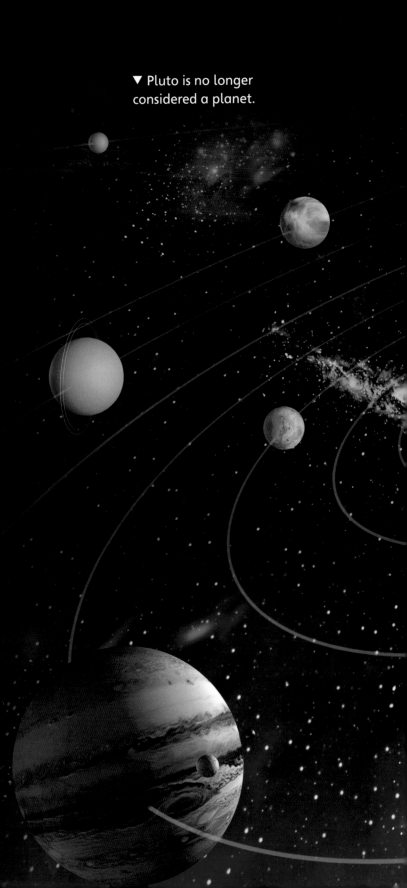

▼ Pluto is no longer considered a planet.

Look at the following chart showing planetary years.

Planet	Year
	365.24 days
	84.07 years
	87.96 days
	164.81 years
	224.68 days
	29.50 years
	686.96 days
	11.86 years

Here is a complete list of the eight planets, in their order from the Sun:

Mercury   Jupiter

Venus   Saturn

Earth   Uranus

Mars   Neptune

Calculation Station

Try matching the correct planet with the given year. Then check your answers in a reference book or on a trustworthy Web site, such as www.nasa.gov. (Answers are on page 31.)

27

Showing Shadows

To try to think like an astronomer, you can study shadows. Have you ever noticed your shadow when you are outside on a sunny day? Have you ever observed that it isn't in the same spot all the time? There is a good reason why it seems as if your shadow moves at different times in the day.

Your shadow, its shape, and where it is on the ground relate to the position of the Sun in the sky. As Earth turns, the Sun seems to move across the sky. With each new position in the sky, your shadow changes length.

In the early morning, the Sun is low in the sky. So your shadow will be long and directly behind you. As the day goes along, the Sun looks like it's higher in the sky but it doesn't move. Your shadow gets shorter. Science—and math—can explain so many of life's puzzles.

◄ Try drawing the Sun and Earth, with lines showing rays reaching Earth, to see which part of Earth is in shadow.

Hands-On Math

You can find an approximate time of the day by using the Sun and shadows.

What You Will Need:

- Flashlight
- Pencil
- Crayon
- Paper
- Tape or glue
- Table or flat desk

What to Do:

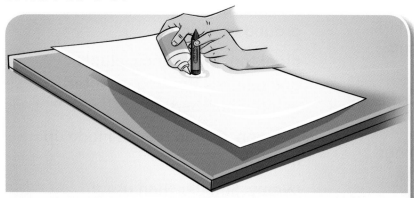

1 Tape or glue the crayon vertically in the middle of the paper.

3 Move the flashlight upward, to model the movement of the Sun toward high noon. Stop the flashlight three times before reaching the high spot overhead. Mark the shadow each time.

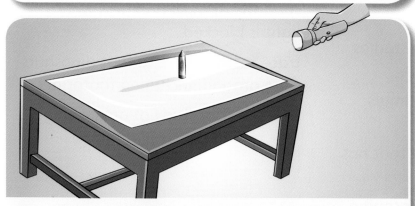

2 Start by shining the flashlight as if it were the Sun rising from one side of the table or desk. Mark the shadow of the crayon.

4 Then move the flashlight downward, toward the opposite side of the desk, to model the Sun setting. Stop the flashlight three times before hitting the sunset. Draw the shadow each time.

Explain Away:

1. *How does the length of your shadow relate to the Sun's position in the sky?*
2. *How can you use your shadow to give you a general idea of what time of day it is?*
   (Answers are on page 31.)

29

Glossary

astronomer Person who studies outer space.

baleen Small strips of a hornlike substance in the mouth of whales.

carnivore Animal that eats only meat.

filter feeder Creature that eats plankton, the tiny plants and animals of the sea.

fossil Remains, like pieces of bone in the ground.

gravity Force that pulls things toward the center of a mass.

hatchling Baby lizards that have just hatched from their eggs.

herbivore Animal that eats only plants.

herpetologist Person who studies reptiles and amphibians.

krill Small crustaceans, animals with shells that bend.

line segment Straight line that has a beginning and an end.

logic Method of correct reasoning.

marine biologist Person who studies life in the water.

omnivore Animal that eats both plants and meat.

paleontologist Person who studies fossils to understand earlier life forms.

parallelogram Four-sided figure with both pairs of opposite sides extended in the same direction, with equal distance between them, and that never meet.

planetary year Length of time needed for a planet to revolve around the Sun.

plankton Microscopic plants and animals floating in water in large numbers.

polygon Closed figures made up of angles.

pygmy Smaller than usual.

ray Line that has no beginning or end.

shadow Area of darkness where light is blocked.

trace fossil Evidence that dinosaurs were around, including footprints.

zoology The study of animals.

Answer Key
Calculation Station

p. 4: 5,700,000 gallons of water ÷ 500 gallons per truck = 11,400 truckloads; 27 trucks × 100 lbs. of salt per truck = 2,700 lbs. of salt.

p. 9: 3 sharks × 2 lbs. fish = 6 lbs. daily; 2 shark × 1.5 lbs. fish = 3 lbs. daily; 6 + 3 = 9 lbs. daily; 9 × 14 days = 126 lbs. daily.

p. 12: 450 lbs. per day × 3 Brachiosaurus = 1,350 lbs. × 3 days = 4,050 lbs. for 3 days; 4,050 lbs. ÷ 50 lbs. = 81 trees.

p. 15: 13,000 pounds ÷ 500 pounds = 35 bites

p. 19: Crocodile: .4 miles in 2 minutes; Alligator: 1.0 miles in 2 minutes; 12 ÷ 60 = .2 × 2 = .4, and 30 ÷ 60 = .5 × 2 = 1.

p. 21: Greens: 16.8 lbs. per 28 days; Vegetable: 16.8 lbs. per 28 days; Fruits and Flowers: 8.4 lbs. per 28 days; 42/ 1 × 2/5 = 84/5 and 42/1 × 1/5 = 42/5 = 8.5.

p. 25: Count the lines. Are there more than three? Look at the angles. Is there a right angle? If you can say "yes" to both questions, the constellation is "right."

p. 27:

Planet	Year
Earth	365.24 days
Uranus	84.07 years
Mercury	87.96 days
Neptune	164.81 years
Venus	224.68 days
Saturn	29.50 years
Mars	686.96 days
Jupiter	11.86 years

Hands-On Math

p. 7: In each case, you divide the length of the whale, in feet, by the height of the individual, in feet. Based on a 4-foot person, the answers would be as follows: Humpback, 10 people; Sperm, 12 people; Blue, 20 people; and Beluga, 30 people.

p. 11:

Whale	Both	Fish
• Warm-blooded • Take care of their young • Smooth skin • Blowhole on top of head • Get oxygen from air • Swim in pods	• Threatened by human fishing • Die if kept out of water • Some make sounds • Found in fresh water and salt water	• Cold-blooded • Do not take care of their young • Scaly skin • Gills on side of head • Get oxygen from water • Swim in schools

p. 17: For the smallest bottle to stand, the legs can be thin. The larger the bottle, the fatter the legs must be. In all cases, it is quite easy to "stand" the bottle on four legs, especially when the legs are the same length. From this, you can see why big dinosaurs had big back legs and why dinosaurs sometimes used all four legs for movement.

p. 23: 1.) 268 crickets; 2.) 4-1/2 c. greens; 3.) $8.04 crickets per 2 weeks; 4.) $0.45 greens per 2 weeks; 5.) $8.49 per 2 weeks; 6.) $8.49 x 2 = $16.98 per month; Mary will not have enough money. She gets $15 monthly, and a lizard costs almost $17.

p. 29: Morning shadows are long and to the right of the crayon; there is no shadow at noon; afternoon shadows are long and to the left.

Index

1-10 J
510
570